MICRO

AUTHORITY

MICRO AUTHORITY

HOW TO ACCELERATE YOUR DISTINCTION IN A CROWDED MARKET IN THE ERA OF SPEED

Dr Raman K. Attri

A Publication of Speed To Proficiency Research: S2Pro©

ISBN: 978-981-18-8054-4 (e-book)
ISBN: 978-981-18-8053-7 (paperback)
ISBN: 978-981-18-8052-0 (hardcover)

Published in Singapore
Printed in the United States of America, Australia, UK

https://www.speedtoproficiency.com
info@speedtoproficiency.com

National Library Board, Singapore Cataloguing in Publication Data

Name(s): Attri, Raman K., 1973-
Title: Micro authority : how to accelerate your distinction in a crowded market in the era of speed / Dr Raman K. Attri.
Description: Singapore : Speed To Proficiency Research, [2023]
Identifier(s): ISBN 978-981-18-8052-0 (hardback) | 978-981-18-8053-7 (paperback) | 978-981-18-8054-4 (e-book)
Subject(s): LCSH: Expertise. | Career development. | Success in business.
Classification: DDC 650.1--dc23

Editor and research: Ms Anjali Alloria

*To my friends and classmates of the 1994 batch
at my grad school, REC/NIT Jalandhar, who
continued to teach me the power of micro-worlds!!*

In the era of speed, your micro-authority determines the pace of your success in a crowded market. Your micro-authority is determined by how well you offer your deep expertise within a specific micro-niche in an unbeatable manner.

AUTHOR

Dr. Raman K. Attri is a sought-after **coach for futuristic chief learning officers** who are ready to stay ahead of their competition. Dr. Attri is the world's leading authority on the "science of speed" in professional learning and performance, with over two decades of research in performance science. His outstanding achievements have earned him recognition as a Brainz Global 500 Leader alongside other stellar personalities such as Oprah Winfrey, Gary Vee, Jim Kwik, and Jim Shetty.

He is a multifaceted personality with a range of talents, including being a scientist, author, speaker, L&D leader, and artist. Despite being permanently disabled since childhood, Dr. Attri is known as a powerhouse of positivity and inspiration. He has transformed his inability to walk into a unique expertise in teaching people how to walk faster in their professional world.

He is the creator of a time-tested, proven system that can help leaders and organizations speed up the path to mastery and leadership in any domain by twofold. His most recent project is the

GetThereFaster portal, a comprehensive resource for anyone seeking to learn the secrets of learning better and faster.

Dr. Attri is a professional speaker who shares research-based insights at leading international conferences with top business executives, helping them to master speed in business, shorten workforce time-to-proficiency, and accelerate employee development.

He is also a global training thought leader at a Fortune 500 technology corporation, managing one of the world's top 10 Hall-of-Fame training organizations.

As the prolific author of 50 multi-genre books, Dr. Attri writes books and articles on various topics ranging from business and leadership to performance and expertise, as well as training and development, HR, and workforce development.

Passionate about continuous learning, Dr. Attri has earned two doctorates in learning, over 100 international educational credentials, several degrees and diplomas, and some of the highest certifications. He is an authentic accelerated learning business coach who practices what he preaches.

Featured in over 125 articles, interviews, and shows, Dr. Attri was awarded as one of the Most Admired Global Indians of 2022. He is a highly sought-after expert whose remarkable achievements continue to inspire everyone he touches to strive for true excellence in their personal and professional lives.

You may contact @DrRamanKAttri on Facebook, LinkedIn, YouTube, Twitter, Instagram, and Tiktok, among other social media platforms. Or visit **https://get-there-faster.com**.

CONTENTS

1

Authority in the Era of Speed

2

Becoming a Great Product in Your Space

3
Clarifying Professional Authority

4
Measuring Professional Authority

5
Accelerating Professional Authority

6

Aligning Two Aspects of Niche

7

Identifying Compelling Micro-Niche

8

Developing Your Micro-Niche Story

9

Career Acceleration Resources

1

Authority in the Era of Speed

"Becoming an authority in your field is a great way to stand out from the competition and position yourself as a go-to thought leader… It all starts with sharing your expertise."

- Liam Austin, Co-Founder at Entrepreneurs HQ

STANDOUT AUTHORITY

In today's fast-paced and ever-evolving business landscape, standing out from the crowd is essential for success. With countless competitors vying for attention and customers, establishing your professional authority has become more critical than ever. But how can you set yourself apart in a crowded marketplace? How can you become the go-to authority in your space? And above all, how can you develop your authority at a much faster pace than the business?

What sets this book apart from other material on authority is its unwavering emphasis on speed and acceleration at every step of the way. As a professional authority on speed in organizational settings, I can vouch that time is the only competitive weapon in this fast-paced world. You need to establish your authority within your space quickly.

This book is specifically tailored to provide you with actionable strategies and practical insights that will expedite your progress. This book is designed to provide you with an accelerated framework to establish unbeatable authority. By going beyond mere expertise and delving into the very essence of authority, this book will equip you with all the tools necessary to dominate your market and become an authority figure.

WHAT TO EXPECT IN THIS BOOK

The journey toward authority begins by understanding what it truly entails. It is not merely a title or a status; it is a combination of various elements that collectively build your credibility, influence, and trustworthiness. This book will explore these elements in depth, ensuring that you have a solid foundation and accurate ways to construct a perceptible authority. The notion of authority is revisited throughout the book to set it apart from expertise, along with the distinctions between authority and personal branding. Once you understand the multiple facets of authority, the book then dives into measurement methods to evaluate and communicate authority.

This book goes beyond theoretical concepts. It provides you with practical approaches, frameworks, and models that will accelerate your process of establishing authority. By embracing these strategies, your journey will be enhanced to become an influential figure in your micro-niche.

This book teaches you the *Product Authority Model*, which focuses on leveraging your unique product or service to establish authority. By understanding how your offering aligns with the needs and desires of your target audience, you can position yourself as the ultimate solution provider in your niche.

Another valuable tool you will learn is the *Professional Authority Model*, which emphasizes the development of your personal brand and expertise. By harnessing your knowledge, experience, and skills, you can create a compelling narrative that highlights your authority in your chosen field.

The book also delves into the *Five Elements of Authority Development* to give you a precise description of which elements to focus on while establishing your professional authority.

To ensure a rapid acceleration of your authority development process, this book introduces the *Professional Authority Acceleration Framework*. This framework is specifically designed to streamline your efforts and guide you through each step with precision and effectiveness. By following this roadmap, you will avoid common pitfalls and overcome obstacles that can hinder your progress.

Furthermore, you will learn to apply the *5-E Thinking Process to Find Your Niche*, a systematic approach that enables you to identify the most favorable micro-niche for your expertise. By evaluating your passions, skills, market demand, and other crucial factors, you can uncover the ideal micro-niche that aligns perfectly with your goals.

Lastly, the book provides you with an *evaluation framework* to assess potential micro-niches and determine the most favorable one for your authority-building journey. This framework will save you time, energy, and resources by enabling you to make informed decisions and focus your efforts on the most promising opportunities.

Throughout these pages, you will find a wealth of knowledge, real-world examples, and actionable advices that will empower you to transform your professional journey. By following the proven strategies outlined in this book, you will elevate your status, build unwavering trust, and become the unbeatable micro-niche authority that your industry demands.

Get ready to embark on a transformative journey toward unrivaled professional authority. Together, let us uncover the keys to your success and set you on a path to dominating your micro-niche like never before. The journey starts now!

2

Becoming a Great Product in Your Space

"To build authority in your niche, you need to sell yourself as a product. This means focusing not only on your skills and expertise but also on your personal brand and how you present yourself to others."

- John Smith, author of "The Art of Micro-Niche Authority

YOU ARE A PRODUCT

I want to challenge you to think about yourself in a different light. As an expert, consultant, manager, or executive, you are not simply a person with a set of skills and knowledge. As Smith also points out, you need to focus on how you present yourself to others.

You are a product

In today's market, it is not enough to simply be an expert in your field. In fact, I would say no; you are not an expert. You have expertise, so you are a product. You need to package yourself in a way that makes you stand out and differentiate yourself from the competition. This can be done by leveraging your skills, knowledge, and expertise to achieve specific goals or solve specific problems.

You are selling yourself

You are not just selling a product; you are the product. You need to understand that you have a unique combination of skills, knowledge, experience, and personality that makes you valuable to your clients. This indicates that you need to be aware of not just your technical skills but also your interpersonal skills, communication skills, and ability to present yourself effectively to potential clients or customers.

Perception is the key

While your expertise and skills are valuable, the perception of your potential clients or customers also plays a crucial role in whether they choose to work with you or not. To become an unbeatable authority, you need to focus on your personal brand and how you present yourself to the world. You need to develop a clear and concise message about what you offer and why you are the best choice for your clients. You need to be authentic and true to yourself while also presenting yourself in a way that resonates with your target audience.

By recognizing that you are a product, you can take control of your personal brand and create a powerful and lasting impression on your clients. So embrace your unique value proposition and let the world know you are an unbeatable authority.

PRODUCT AUTHORITY MODEL

As someone who has spent over 15 to 20 years in the product development industry, working with some of the best tech organizations, and having been a product design scientist for over a decade, I have gained a deep understanding of the philosophy behind product development. Through this experience, I have come to realize that successful products always have strong authority in the market. The success of a product is heavily reliant on its ability to establish an unbeatable micro-niche authority in the market. This can be achieved by focusing on three key elements: Product, position, and perception.

Figure 1: Product Authority Model

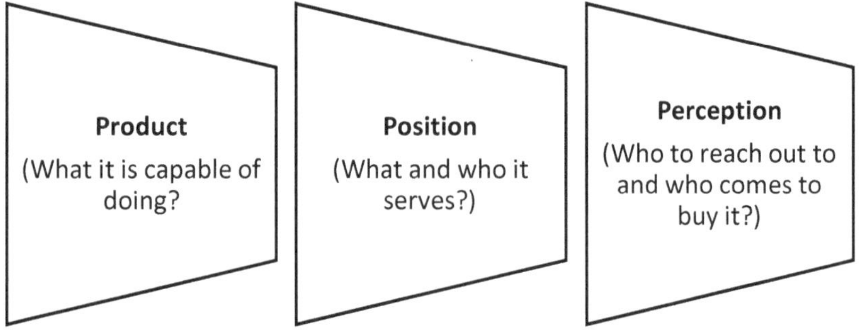

Product: What is the product capable of doing?

The product's unique features and capabilities must set it apart from other similar products on the market. It should be able to perform certain tasks that other products cannot, effectively satisfying the needs of the target audience. For example, the iPhone's internet access capability revolutionized the smartphone industry and appealed to customers who were seeking this feature.

Position: What and who will the product serve?

Positioning is an important aspect of establishing product authority. Don Norman, director of The Design Lab at the University of California, San Diego, states, "*The best products are designed with the user in mind, and they are a joy to use.*"

A product authority model is used by product designers or scientists to determine the niche market in which the product will serve. The product should be designed to cater to the specific needs of the target audience, positioning itself in such a way that it serves them well and matches their requirements. For example, the iPhone was positioned as a high-end smartphone, catering to the needs of professionals and executives.

Perception: Who to reach out to and who comes to buy it?

Perception is the key factor that contributes to the success of a product in the market. It is shaped by its marketing and branding efforts, and it is essential to ensure that the product is marketed in a way that appeals to the target audience. For example, the iPhone's branding was outstanding, which helped create a positive perception among customers and contributed to its success in the market.

In conclusion, all three elements must work together to establish an unbeatable micro-niche authority for a product. By catering to a specific and targeted audience, understanding their needs, and creating a unique and memorable brand identity, a product can establish itself as an expert in that particular area and gain a loyal following, leading to its success in the market.

MAKING OF A GREAT PRODUCT

If you are convinced that you are a product, then you first need to understand the basics of the *Product Authority Model*. Let's first start with what makes a product great.

Let's take the example of the iPhone, which undoubtedly is a great product due to its extraordinary breakthroughs. How does the iPhone stand out as one of the greatest products and establish its authority over other brands or models?

The key to the iPhone being a great product lies in its ability to serve a specific niche, desiring a specific purpose. It offers unique features and functions that set it apart from other products, making it highly successful. What offers its authority as an exceptional product is not just its performance, but also the ability to hardly replicate while keeping the product's integrity intact.

Chris Pearson states, "*Good products are built on a foundation of doing ordinary things extraordinarily well.*" Table 1 states five reasons to consider why products like iPhones are considered world-class and exceptional.

Table 1: Five characteristics of a great product

A great product	Never-seen-before features in a niche
	Unparalleled hold on the market
	Distinctive standout branding
	Impeccably designed and well documented
	Unbeatable value proposition

Never-seen-before features

While there is no scarcity of brilliant smartphones in the industry, what set the iPhone apart was that it brought about unprecedented innovation at a time when specific features, such as the touchscreen, were not available elsewhere. By introducing the touchscreen, the iPhone transformed the way users interact with their phones. This pioneering development has replaced physical buttons with intuitive gestures and touch, thereby redefining the user experience.

The iPhone also opened up the users' world by providing access to the entire internet, something that set a new standard for mobile technology. Thus, by expanding the possibilities of communication and information sharing, it forever changed the role of smartphones in the modern man's world.

As professionals in micro-niche industries, we must take note of this phenomenon and constantly push the boundaries of what is possible to establish ourselves as authorities in our field. In doing so, we can develop a reputation as innovative leaders who set the standard for professional excellence.

Unparalleled hold on the market

The iPhone has established itself as an unparalleled success in the consumer electronics industry, commanding a substantial market share and creating a frenzy among consumers. Its soaring demand and high price point have transformed it into a coveted status symbol, embodying the pinnacle of technological innovation and style. The reason the iPhone continues to have a powerful driving force in the market even to this day is because of its ability to not only create but also sustain consumer demand in the market by constantly re-innovating.

Distinctive standout branding

The iPhone is a great product not only because it serves its audience in unique ways and captures the market, but also owing to its unmatched expertise in developing a standout brand identity. From a globally recognizable Apple logo to the sleek and sophisticated design, the iPhone's branding sets it apart from all other phones on the market. This distinctive branding is a combination of premium quality, user experience, innovation, branding consistency, and lifestyle branding that has helped to establish the iPhone as a highly desirable product in the smartphone industry.

Impeccably designed and documented

The iPhone was impeccably well-designed, making it easy for users to operate and understand. The fact that the phone was so intuitive and user-friendly was a major selling point and helped make the iPhone a success. What also added to its success was its thought leader, Steve Jobs, who would often highlight the iPhone's design, features, and functionality during product launches and presentations to show how the device was innovative and different from its competitors. The iPhone's design was so meticulously crafted that it has become an iconic symbol of innovation and sophistication.

Unbeatable value proposition

The iPhone's supreme value proposition in the smartphone industry offers its users an all-in-one solution with unprecedented convenience and simplicity. Its single-button design, combined with its ability to consolidate a wide range of functions into one device, was a game-changer for the mobile phone market. This unique value proposition not only set the iPhone apart from its competitors but also helped to create an entirely new market segment. The iPhone's ability to provide an effortless and comprehensive user experience has played a crucial role in making it one of the most successful and recognizable products in the world.

The iPhone's remarkable success is rooted in these five essential characteristics that have established it as an unmatched authority model in the crowded smartphone market. These characteristics have contributed to the iPhone's enduring influence and its ongoing impact on consumer culture worldwide.

The iPhone's model provides a blueprint for establishing oneself as an authority in any professional field, offering valuable lessons on the importance of branding, design, market appeal, and sustained demand in achieving lasting success. Here I also attempted to map out a model that can help you get there faster and stand apart within your respective micro-niche.

PROFESSIONAL AUTHORITY MODEL

Now, if you are a product, how will your professional authority look as a product? The answer lies in the *Professional Authority Model*. Assuming that you are a product, there are three key components to your professional authority, as shown Fig. 2.

Figure 2: Professional Authority Model

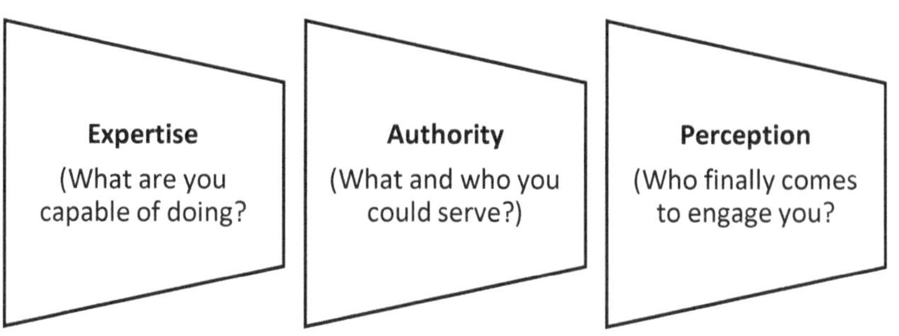

Expertise: What are you capable of doing?

This refers to your unique set of skills, knowledge, and capabilities that set you apart from others in the market. Your expertise is what makes you valuable and sought-after, just like a product's features.

Authority: What and who could you serve?

Building authority means leveraging your expertise to provide solutions, advice, and support to others in your industry or market. It is not enough to simply have expertise; you need to take it outside of yourself and make it useful for others. This will enhance your reputation and credibility, helping you establish yourself as an authority in your field.

Perception: Who will engage with what you have to offer?

Perception is how the market apprehends your expertise and authority. It is influenced by various factors such as marketing, branding, and reputation within your industry or market. It determines those individuals who will ultimately consume and benefit from your expertise and authority.

It is crucial to understand that authority is not about being an authority for the entire world; rather, it involves becoming an authority within a specific niche audience that you serve. For instance, a surgeon can establish authority within the medical field by saving lives and making a significant impact.

When you view yourself as a product and focus on developing your professional authority, you can embark on a journey that leads to success and fulfillment in your career.

MAKING OF AN AUTHORITY

Developing professional and personal authority is no different from establishing a product's authority in the market. Like a great product, your authority is also characterized by five equivalent elements, which represent a system called the *Accelerated Authority Development Framework*. These elements are shown in Table 2 and listed here:

1. *Micro-niche*: A deeper and narrow expertise in a micro-niche
2. *Niche Market*: A niche market segment or audience
3. *Standout impression*: Highly differentiated personal branding
4. *Tangible wisdom*: Unique wisdom documented or modeled
5. *Value proposition*: Unbeatable value proposition

Table 2: A great product versus great authority

A great product	A great authority
Never-seen-before features in a niche	**Micro-niche:** A deeper and narrow expertise in a micro-niche
Unparalleled hold on the market	**Niche Market:** A niche market segment or audience

Distinctive standout branding	**Standout impression:** Highly differentiated personal branding
Impeccably designed and well documented	**Tangible wisdom:** Unique wisdom documented or modeled
Unbeatable value proposition	**Value proposition:** Unbeatable value proposition

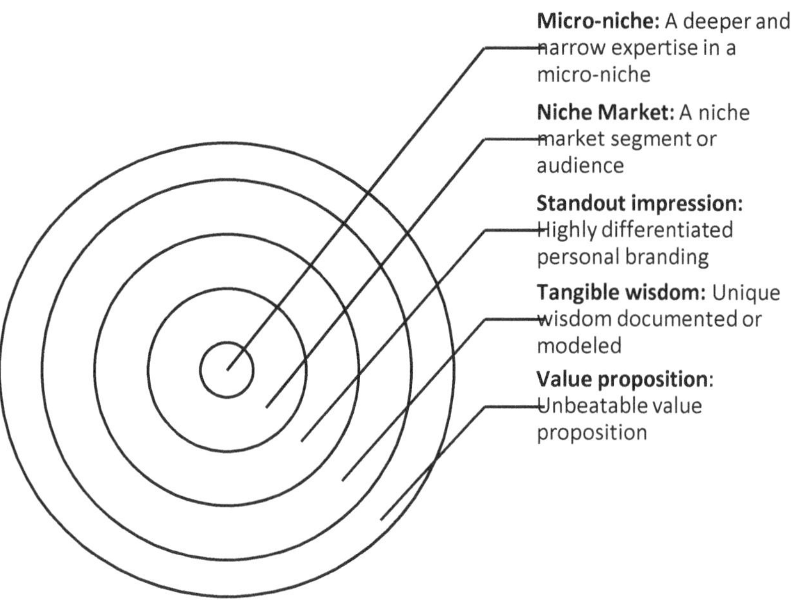

Figure 3: Five elements of the Accelerated Professional Authority Development Framework

Here are five elements within this system:

Deeper and narrow expertise micro-niche

In today's saturated market, positioning yourself to a broader niche is no longer viable, as every niche is becoming easily replaceable and imitable, irrespective of the profession you might find yourself in. There is a pressing need to identify the "unique you," in the form of your specific set of skills or expertise in a micro-niche. A micro-niche is within a specific field where you can stand apart from the rest.

Consequently, the foremost element of a powerful, distinctive authority is to identify your micro-niche—which is basically a niche within a niche. It is a highly specific area where you excel and stand out, where you genuinely believe you are the best, where others acknowledge your expertise, or where you have evidence of your exceptional capabilities.

When I started, I initially thought that Learning and Development was a niche, but I was mistaken, as it has become a vast domain with a multitude of professionals. Therefore, within the wider domain of learning and development, I delineated my niche as "designing complex learning." However, soon I realized that there were thousands of others within this niche too. Then, to set myself apart from the rest, I had to position myself in the micro-niche of "speeding up the process of complex learning," which requires specific kinds of techniques to design learning. Few professionals in the market claim to have expertise in this aspect, making it my unique micro-niche. The moment I positioned myself there, I was able to translate my expertise into something that stood out quickly.

To truly differentiate yourself, you need to go beyond the wider domain and find your micro-niche. It will set you apart from the competition and narrow down your focus. Sally Hogshead states in Fascinate: Your 7 Triggers to Persuasion and Captivation: "*Find your micro niche by identifying the unique qualities and insights that set you apart from others; be bold in claiming your space, and others will recognize your expertise.*"

Eric Ries, in The Lean Startup: How Today's Entrepreneurs Use Continuous Innovation to Create Radically Successful Businesses, states, "*Developing your niche requires deep introspection and a willingness to experiment; take risks, learn from failures, and constantly iterate your approach.*" As Eric Ries aptly highlights, this process requires willingness, introspection, and effective risk-taking. Identifying and embracing your micro-niche is crucial for establishing your authority. It may limit your field of expertise, but it will position you as an unparalleled expert in that specific area. By honing your micro-niche, you create a distinct identity and solidify your position as a leader in your field.

While establishing your micro-niche, keep in mind that it is not your profession. Your niche is independent of your job, profession, or education. An example could be a specialist in a specific type of medical procedure while also being a medical surgeon by profession.

Niche segment, market, or audience

When you have a well-defined micro-niche, it becomes crucial to target a specific niche market that can truly benefit from your expertise. Trying to cater to everyone can dilute your impact and hinder your ability to make a significant mark. To sustain your authority within a micro-niche, it is crucial for your highly specific skills and expertise to be aligned with a target audience.

Gary Vaynerchuk states in Jab, Jab, Jab, Right Hook: How to Tell Your Story in a Noisy Social World: "*To accelerate your niche… connect with your audience, and become an influential voice in your space.*" This niche market or audience will be that group of people who value and respect your expertise and have a true need for what you are offering. So, instead of trying to serve everyone, you must focus on your target audience (individuals and organizations) who are most likely to value and utilize our offerings effectively.

This targeted approach enables us to optimize our efforts and maximize our impact within a specific market segment. By understanding and catering to the unique needs of our niche audience, we can position ourselves as valuable and sought-after experts, leading to increased opportunities for success.

For instance, my niche market within my micro-niche is that set of audience that is looking to master complex skills within a shorter timeframe and speed up their process of becoming an authority within its respective field.

Your niche segment or audience need not be about developing a huge following. It could be a small group of people who need your unique skills or knowledge, or a wider audience that is interested in your area of expertise. For example, a financial advisor who specializes in helping retirees plan their retirement may have a specific niche segment or audience.

Highly differentiated personal branding

The third crucial element is creating a standout impression that sets your expertise apart from the competition. As Tim Ferriss, in The 4-Hour Workweek: Escape 9-5, Live Anywhere, and Join the New Rich, highlights that it is essential to make a lasting impression that distinguishes you as a unique and unparalleled authority in your field. He says: "*Authority and expertise are the currency of your personal brand; it is through the strategic cultivation and presentation of both that you create an impactful and lasting impression.*"

This can be achieved through various effective marketing strategies and features that showcase your expertise in a remarkable way. By leveraging innovative and distinctive approaches, you can ensure that your impression resonates with your target audience, leaving an indelible mark that sets you apart from others.

Among all things, personal strategic branding is key to conveying authority. Dorie Clark emphasized in Stand Out: How to Find Your Breakthrough Idea and Build a Following Around It: "*Authority, expertise, and personal branding are interwoven; your expertise builds your authority, and your personal brand is the vehicle that showcases both to the world.*"

Through strategic branding, compelling content, exceptional service, and impactful communication, you can establish a reputation that is matchless and unrivaled. It is through these standout impressions that you create a powerful presence and cultivate a sense of exclusivity that attracts and captivates your audience, solidifying your position as a true authority.

It is your unique personal branding that ultimately makes you stand apart from others in your field. For instance, a motivational speaker known for his energetic and charismatic personality is a good example of personal branding.

However, personal branding is often misconstrued when it is articulated as an identity built around one element of overall existence, which tends to be an incomplete picture. To establish oneself as an authority, there is a need to showcase your unique multidimensional personality, consisting of a holistic gamut of your skills, knowledge, and everything else that makes you a complete package.

Unique wisdom documented or modeled

Part of developing authority within a niche involves transforming your expertise into something concrete and accessible. As Robert Cialdini stated in Influence: The Psychology of Persuasion, *"Influence is built through the combination of knowledge, credibility, and generosity. Share your wisdom freely, and others will seek it out."*

Nonetheless, rather than letting your ideas float in the abstract, it is crucial to document and share this wisdom in various forms. This requires creating collateral materials that exhibit your wisdom and serve as valuable resources for others. These materials can include books, articles, videos, or a series of informative content.

By creating these resources, you establish yourself as an authority figure with a wealth of valuable insights. These resources not only solidify your authority but also provide a means for others to benefit from your accumulated wisdom. Remember, it is through the expression and sharing of your wisdom leave a lasting impression and establish you as a trusted source in your niche. As Cialdini says, once you share this wisdom, you will attract the right niche audience that is seeking that wisdom, thus solidifying your authority within your micro-niche.

In order to stand out in a crowded market, it is not only important to have a unique offering and audience, but your wisdom should also be teachable. It should be grounded in research, experience, or observation and be easily graspable by others. That also means it should be documented or modeled. This documentation can take the form of books, videos, or other materials consisting of well-framed, clear, and concise methods. For example, a chef who has developed a unique cooking method and documented it in a cookbook can be considered an authority in his field.

Unbeatable Value proposition

The final component of establishing authority lies in crafting an unbeatable value proposition that sets the individual apart from others. This is especially crucial in the space of a micro-niche with highly specialized offerings, where a unique value proposition can become the reason the niche audience picks you over others. You need something so powerful that, the moment it is laid out, you are already distinguished from others in your field. Pat Flynn says in Will It Fly? How to Test Your Next Business Idea So You Don't Waste Your Time and Money, *"Micro-authority is about identifying and owning your unique value proposition, then using that to build credibility and trust."*

This proposition should be so compelling and unique that no one else can come close to matching it. Its significance cannot be emphasized enough. My personal value proposition is that I invite my audience to pay for the results they would achieve through the mentoring process, not the process itself. I offer a value proposition of reducing your journey time by 50% or your money back guarantee. This claim sets a high bar for others in my micro-niche to match. If they attempt to approach this claim, it becomes highly challenging for them to surpass or replicate it. A personal coach offering a money-back guarantee if his clients do not achieve their desired results in a certain time period is an example of a powerful value proposition. Therefore, the value proposition plays a pivotal role in establishing and sustaining authority.

Hence, the value proposition should be unique, unrivaled, and provide a strong reason for people to choose the individual over others in a particular field. Though, your value proposition is linked to the audience you serve. Jay Baer, author, Hall-of-Fame keynote speaker, and founder of Convince & Convert, states, *"Identifying and understanding your target audience is the first step toward delivering value and meeting their needs."*

AUTHORITY DEVELOPMENT

Here is a guidance tool to help you reflect upon five elements of authority development.

Table 3: Summary of five elements of the Accelerated Authority Development Framework

Element	Represents	Definition
Micro-niche	What do I do?	Professional micro-niche, which is unique and exceptional
Niche market	Who do I serve?	Market that values, respects, and chases after you
Standout impression	How do I look?	Branding, impression, and story that set you apart from the crowd
Tangible wisdom	How do I serve?	Well-documented wisdom (or experience) that can be modeled and presented
Value preposition	Why me?	Unbeatable value preposition or transformational promise that no one can match

Micro-niche - What do I do? What is my unique and exceptional professional micro-niche?

Niche market - Who do I sell? What is the market that values, respects, and chooses me?

Standout impression - How do I look out there, either on the stage, on social media, in the market, or in other places? What is the branding, impression, and story that set me apart from the crowd?

Tangible Wisdom - How do I serve and share my wisdom? Do I have well-documented wisdom (or experience) that can be modeled and presented?

Value proposition - Why me? What is my unbeatable value proposition or transformational promise that no one can match?

Once you have these five elements defined, you can establish yourself as the authority within your micro-niche. In my case, brooding over these five factors allows me to be recognized as an authority figure capable of reducing individuals' time by 50% and helping them accelerate their progress toward their goals. This is how expertise in learning faster evolves into authority in the realm of speed.

TIP: BUILD VISIBLE AUTHORITY

It all comes down to how you can accelerate setting yourself up as the professional authority within your micro-niche by honing the power of establishing visibly perceived authority. This process can be sped up when you understand the intricacies of a great product, recognize yourself as a product, and translate your internal expertise into a perceptibly experienced professional authority.

3

Clarifying Professional Authority

"Authority is not a destination, but a journey. Embrace the process, and remember that every step you take brings you closer to becoming a world-class leader."

- Simon Sinek, Start with Why: How Great Leaders Inspire Everyone to Take Action

In order to set yourself apart as a go-to authority in the crowded marketplace, it is critical to first clarify professional authority, especially in the ways this notion differs from the conventional understanding of authority. Thus, this process of clarifying professional authority is one that you can adapt to your professional life, irrespective of the position you occupy.

YOUR BRAND AUTHORITY IS NOT YOUR AUTHORITY

In today's world, people follow personalities, not just brands or companies. When there is sufficient trust in a leader, trust in his vision or product inevitably follows. Take the example of Elon Musk and Tesla. When you follow Elon Musk, you follow him as an authority in his field, his beliefs, his goals, and his professional authority. You may not even know the Tesla logo, but you recognize Elon Musk. This is the power of building professional authority. John C. Maxwell, an American author, rightly stated that "*People buy into the leader before they buy into the vision.*" Thus, as professionals, we need to focus on establishing our professional authority rather than just promoting our brand or company. Building professional authority means displaying your unique set of skills, knowledge, and personality that make you valuable to your clients or customers. This is what makes people want to follow you, not just your brand or company.

So, before you spend millions of dollars in marketing your brand or company, invest in building your professional authority. Take inspiration from thought leaders like Elon Musk, Bill Gates, and others who have established their professional authority and carry it with them wherever they go. Remember, people follow people, and building professional authority is key to becoming an unbeatable micro-niche authority. The more you build your professional authority, the more valuable you become as a product in the market.

The example of Elon Musk and Tesla brings us to the following crucial ideas that can help begin the process of characterizing professional authority:

Use your expertise as a product

Your expertise, wisdom, and knowledge can be seen as a product that can be sold and marketed. View yourself as a product and focus on building your professional authority.

Focus on professional authority

Focus on building professional authority rather than just promoting your business or brand. This authority is portable and can be taken to any company or profession you join in the future.

People follow people

People follow people, not brands or logos. Focus on building professional authority to increase your value as a product in the market.

With these three cornerstones laid down, it becomes easier to envision the process of establishing professional authority. This is further streamlined by the Professional Authority Model.

PERSONAL BRANDING IS NOT AUTHORITY

Contrary to conventional wisdom, building a personal brand should not be the initial focus. Instead, nurturing and harnessing your professional authority will naturally shape your personal brand, amplifying your impact across various domains. The key lies in understanding that your authority becomes the driving force behind your personal brand, just like how Elon Musk's insurmountable authority drives his personal brand for ventures including Tesla, Hyperloop, and Mars missions.

In the pursuit of establishing micro-niche authority, it is vital to understand that your professional authority takes precedence over personal branding. By prioritizing and cultivating your authority, you unlock limitless possibilities, enabling you to leave an enduring mark across diverse ventures and endeavors. Embracing this approach empowers you to make a meaningful difference, transcending the bounds of personal branding.

By adopting this paradigm, remarkable achievements become attainable. Your authority will position you shoulder-to-shoulder with renowned leaders, just as I have been featured on the same forums with names like Les Brown and even luminaries like Bill Clinton. As a performance scientist and transformational leader, I am frequently sought after and highlighted on various prominent platforms, despite maintaining a minimal social media presence. The reason is that I prioritize professional authority over personal branding. Personal branding follows from authority you build. Just as I have been starred on esteemed magazine covers and recognized as a global 500 leader by Brainz magazine alongside influential figures like Oprah Winfrey, Gary Vee, Jim Kwik, and others, you too can rise to eminence.

EXPERTISE IS NOT AUTHORITY

Expertise is something that you possess or are capable of. Chris Brogan said, *"Expertise is what you have; authority is what they perceive you to have."* How expertise is perceived and serves others is what distinguishes it from authority.

A surgeon or doctor may have extensive medical expertise and knowledge, but their authority comes from the recognition and trust they receive from their patients and colleagues. They are considered authorities in their field because of their ability to serve the needs of their patients and the trust they have earned from the medical community. For further elaboration, consider a surgeon who walks into a room, examines a patient, reviews a few vital statistics, and confidently declares, "Surgery is necessary." This internal knowledge of medicine, when put into practice, is labeled as expertise. This particular characteristic demonstrates the surgeon's capabilities.

However, does this alone make that surgeon an authority? Although he may possess exceptional surgical abilities and be adept at diagnosing patients, true authority has not yet been attained.

To establish true authority, observable or recognized metrics or key performance indicators (KPIs) need to be associated with it. In other words, authority becomes evident when we can identify apparent outcomes.

In the case of a surgeon, his authority is established through a history of successful and flawless operations, as well as the lives he has saved. These measurable achievements serve as the metrics or KPIs that bring recognition from other hospitals, invitations from universities to educate their students, and opportunities to present their experiences at esteemed conferences.

In other words, expertise is an internal quality, while authority is external. It is crucial to remember that authority must be visibly recognized by others. Without this visibility, you may still have expertise, but you are not considered an authority in your field. While expertise is an essential foundation, authority is achieved when tangible outcomes and recognized achievements are associated with it. It is the combination of expertise and demonstrated success that elevates individuals to the status of authorities in their respective fields.

Daniel Goleman, a psychologist and the author of Emotional Intelligence, says, "*Expertise is a personal attribute; authority is a recognized status.*" It is crucial to grasp the distinction between expertise and authority. While your expertise represents your technical proficiency in a particular field, it does not automatically enable you to command authority. This distinction may prove challenging for many to follow. Often, people tend to overemphasize their expertise without effectively communicating and establishing their authority in their respective fields. This can result in limited financial success, a lack of opportunities to showcase their expertise, and difficulty selling their products or services. The issue arises when individuals focus solely on promoting their expertise without taking the necessary steps to establish their authority visibly.

In our professional journeys, our managers, leaders, and the corporate world often emphasize sharpening our expertise. However, it is important to recognize that expertise is something we already possess, and further sharpening may yield diminishing returns. The true focus should be on sharpening our authority. This distinction can be better understood through the following three principles:

Table 4: Distinction between expertise and authority

	Expertise	Authority
Meaning	What do you have?	What does the world get?
Reach	What are you capable of doing?	Who and how do you serve their needs?
Disposition	Internal to you	External to you
Visibility	Must be deeply experienced by	Must be visible and noticed by others

Authority is outward-facing

Expertise is an internal quality; it is something that an individual possesses and has the capability to do. On the other hand, authority is expertise made visible externally; it is the recognition and trust that people have in an individual's ability to solve their problems. Authority is what others see and experience from an individual.

Authority must be visible

Authority must be visible; it must be seen by others. If it is not visible, it is not seen and, thus, not considered authority. The visibility of authority can come from various sources, such as word of mouth, online presence, media coverage, etc. This also ties in with the previously elaborated notion of well-designed and documented products that are very visibly present in the market within your micro-niche audience.

Expertise needs to be translated into authority intentionally

Often, people focus on promoting their expertise and overlook the importance of translating it into visible authority. Merely projecting one's expertise does not necessarily translate it into authority. It actually requires a combination of expertise and the ability to solve people's problems effectively and consistently. Overselling expertise without a corresponding manifestation of authority can lead to a lack of recognition and opportunities.

PROFESSIONAL TITLE IS NOT AUTHORITY

Jim Collins stated in Good to Great, "*Authority is not a title, but a mindset; embrace learning, growth, and collaboration to truly lead.*" This is what the changing ideology of authority reflects. It is no longer established outside of the limited frame of titles, positions of leadership, or owning a business, contrary to what the world of business and expertise would lead you to believe. Rather, this notion of authority is a quality that expands beyond titles and can be accessed and commanded through a wide range of sources.

For instance, an employee possessing a wealth of knowledge and expertise in a specific field can personify this quality of authority. A leadership role is not necessarily a prerequisite to commanding authority. In the same breath, being a leader does not necessarily endow someone with authority automatically. This quality of professional authority can be commanded by an expert in a particular field solely on account of their expertise, regardless of their leadership position.

According to this conception of authority as a quality emerging from expertise, skills, experience, and contributions to the respective professional domains, even solution providers, vendors, researchers, and scientists can demonstrate this quality of authority.

SPEEDING UP AUTHORITY DEVELOPMENT

In order to speed up your journey to setting yourself apart as an authority in your professional micro-niche, you need absolute clarity on what makes a professional authority and what does not. The key lies in focusing on genuine authority rather than just seeking visibility. When you prioritize becoming a "true authority" within your field rather than solely aiming to be seen as an authority by a larger audience, you fast-track your journey toward becoming a highly enviable world-class authority.

While the five elements discussed previously are the foundation of the authority framework, you should stay clear of traditional philosophies like personal branding as a symbol of authority or vice versa. At the same time, your success on social media is also not an indication of true authority. This clarity is a powerful accelerator for speed. In the end, as Eric Ries stated in The Lean Startup, "*Speeding up authority requires the ability to adapt and pivot; being agile and responsive to change will accelerate your growth as a leader.*"

4

Measuring Professional Authority

"Becoming a world-class authority requires not only mastering your field, but also understanding how to communicate your expertise effectively to others."

- Susan Cain, Quiet: The Power of Introverts in a World That Can't Stop Talking

You can become a lionized authority at a faster rate if you are clear about the indicators and measurements of "True Authority."

BECOMING A TRUE AUTHORITY

Why can't you establish authority faster, or why does it take too long? The fundamental issue lies in the excessive focus on sharpening expertise while neglecting the development of authority. This is a common problem in the corporate cycle: Individuals spend significant time honing their expertise but fail to invest in cultivating their authority.

Another culprit is misguided coaching, which emphasizes building a *perceived authority* instead of developing into a true expert. Such coaching encourages individuals to prioritize things like social media posting and personal branding as a means to establish authority. However, this approach rarely accelerates the journey toward becoming a top-notch authority. In fact, scientific evidence suggests that such practices do not contribute to authority significantly.

The reason for this misguided coaching is that most consultants or influencers lack the knowledge and expertise to shorten the time required to attain expertise in any profession. Accelerating the time to expertise demands a specialized system and a scientific approach. It necessitates the establishment of true authority, not just its appearance.

The critical question to contemplate is: Do you aim to be perceived as an authority, or do you strive to be a true authority? There is a distinct difference between the two. To become a true authority, you must have outcome metrics or KPIs that demonstrate your expertise. These KPIs serve as the foundation of your authority.

Let's consider some examples:

Nas Daily, a well-known social media influencer and video maker, established his authority through his KPI of producing one-minute storytelling videos each day. He did not rely merely on his millions of followers. Anyone can gain followers, but not everyone can have outcomes as unique as Nas' because it is his command over authority within his micro-niche that sets him apart.

Les Brown, a legendary motivational speaker, defined his authority by his KPI of motivating millions by giving speeches to a stadium full of people who wanted to listen to him, even without having thousands of followers.

Elon Musk, the world's richest businessperson and founder of Tesla, did not base his authority on his tweets to followers but rather on the KPI of his unique desire to put a man on Mars, a goal that no one else can parallel.

None of these individuals focused solely on being perceived as authorities. They prioritized the attainment of unique outcomes and established their authority through tangible achievements.

Therefore, the real question to ponder is - do you want to 'be' a real authority or do you want to be 'seen' as an authority?

MEASURING AUTHORITY

Now, the crucial question arises: How can we effectively measure authority to communicate our expertise?

While people often measure expertise based on factors such as years of experience or notable accomplishments, measuring authority requires a different approach. Measurement becomes essential to assess your position and progress throughout the authority journey.

Imagine organizing a prestigious conference where you cannot invite every expert in the field. Instead, you rely on specific metrics to identify the outstanding authorities in that space. How would you measure or compare one expert's authority with the others? What metrics would you consider for this assessment?

Irrespective of the field or domain, a person's authority is validated by external recognition. It involves evaluating tangible indicators that reflect the recognition and impact you have in your field. It is through these measures that your authority becomes evident, solidifying your position as a trusted and respected authority figure.

Put yourself on the receiving end, as if you were the one to get invited as an authority to such a conference. How would you quantify your authority? What are the outcomes or metrics you have delivered or can produce that prove you are an authority in that domain or topic?

Depending on your industry or profession, you can measure it through various indicators such as followers, video views, subscribers, or the number of users engaging with your app. These metrics signify the trust and influence you hold, as people choose to follow and use your services due to your perceived authority.

In the speaking, training, and consulting industries, a significant measure is media coverage. Being consistently invited for magazine features, podcast interviews, or TV appearances reflects your established authority. This sets you apart from the vast pool of experts, highlighting your distinctive expertise that resonates with others.

In academic circles, researchers' authority is often determined by the number of citations their papers receive. A higher citation count signifies greater research authority and proficiency. Conferences and speaking opportunities further affirm authority as organizers approach those individuals who have already demonstrated visible authority through their mentions and citations.

In the case of the construction project management industry, a project manager's authority can be assessed through various metrics. One needs to consider the scale of the projects successfully handled and the cycle time required. You might consider factors such as the number of projects completed over the past decade, the substantial cost savings achieved for owners, or even the record-breaking speed of erecting a building. For instance, in China, a building was constructed in just 36 hours. The project manager responsible for such an achievement would undoubtedly be regarded as an authority due to these measurable metrics.

However, many of these factors primarily exist within internal reports. The challenge lies in making these metrics visible to those who need to recognize your authority.

In the case of the tech industry, how can you establish and communicate your authority in this domain? What metrics and measurements will you employ? Perhaps you have not given this much thought before.

If you aspire to establish your authority - ***You need to think about your measurement, you will need to measure yourself.*** You need to carefully consider the metrics that will validate your expertise and convey your authority to others. It is important to note that your boss or employer may have their own unique criteria for measuring your performance, which should be considered alongside your broader authority-building efforts.

DEFINING AUTHORITY METRICS

Without measuring your authority, you cannot rightfully claim the title. It is through measurement that you gain awareness of your position along the journey of authority. Therefore, it is essential to precisely quantify your authority.

Let's consider the example of my friend Rakesh Puril, a web security expert in a renowned security firm in New Jersey. His authority metrics lie in the number of complex web attacks he has successfully thwarted and the monetary value he has saved by doing so. These tangible KPIs effectively convert his expertise into authority.

How often do we give thought to these authority metrics? Take a moment to reflect on your profession, whether you are in the tech industry or construction management. What specific KPIs or indicators will you produce that will explicitly demonstrate your status as an authority? It is crucial to approach this question without the context of social media metrics and follower counts. Bernard Marr, an international bestselling business author, says, *"Without KPIs, it is like navigating a ship without a compass."*

In a crowded marketplace, it is essential to identify the KPIs that establish your micro-niche authority and differentiate you from the competition. As Bernard Marr rightly highlights, you need a KPI to navigate your journey toward establishing authority, and to measure it. It is time to reflect on your own authority metrics and consider how they translate your expertise into true authority.

What sets authorities like Nas Daily, Les Brown, or Elon Musk apart? Why do they possess authority? The answer lies in their ability to produce outcomes that hold present significance and future leverage. Nas Daily, for example, continually builds new businesses, leveraging his authority through the outcomes he has achieved. His remarkable upshot of amassing millions of subscribers serves as a testament to his authority. Thus, when measuring your own authority, focus on the outcomes you have generated, as they become an enduring part of your identity and shape your future potential.

For instance, I personally hold two doctorates and possess 100 international credentials, achievements that will forever accompany me and offer leverage in any future endeavors. Once you have established your authority by measuring your outcomes, it is an asset that will live with you forever.

Table 5: Examples of metrics or KPIs for authority measurement

Role	Metrics/KPIs
Influencer	Followers, subscribers, video views
Business person	Revenue generated
Founder	Number of platform users
Speakers	Media features, speeches delivered
Author	Citations, mentions
Researchers	Citations

By identifying and refining your authority metrics, you can establish a clear path toward becoming a recognized authority within your micro-niche. It is through the cultivation of these metrics that you will differentiate yourself, gain credibility, and solidify your position as an influential figure. Effectively measuring authority allows you to communicate its value effectively.

TIP: PRIOTIZE METRICS

This systematic approach is essential for effectively measuring your professional authority and communicating your value to others. By understanding the importance of external validation and tangible metrics, you can showcase your expertise and distinguish yourself in your field. Once you define the metrics or KPIs that signify your authority, you can develop a roadmap in terms of milestones. These milestones will represent how you want to see your metrics or KPIs grow over time as you scale new heights. Remember, at every milestone, measuring your authority is the key to attaining a sense of achievement, effectively communicating your value, and establishing yourself as a respected authority figure.

5

Accelerating Professional Authority

In previous chapters, we explored the elements that contribute to establishing authority. Let's now delve into an equally important question: How can you accelerate your journey to becoming an authority?

The authority acceleration framework is described using the outcome-time graph in this figure. We plot time on the horizontal axis, while the vertical axis represents the outcomes that define authority, as authority is measured by the tangible results you produce.

Figure 4: Authority-Time growth graph

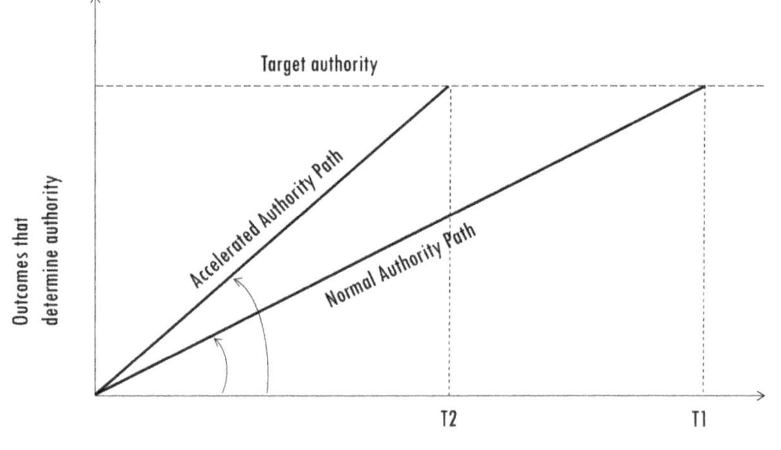

The bottom curve on the chart, denoted as 'normal authority path,' represents the typical progression of individuals toward their target level of authority, shown by the dotted line 'target authority.' It is a qualified indicator, say 1000 subscribers to your services as an outcome. You may take a certain number of years, say T1, to reach there. However, if you aim to get there faster and achieve authority more swiftly, say in time T2, you need an accelerator—a mechanism that propels you forward. Such a mechanism needs to develop your authority at a higher slope, as depicted by the 'accelerated authority path.'

Now, let's analyze the chart and identify any gears or levers we can manipulate to enhance our acceleration toward authority. There are five levers or parameters that can help achieve this goal.

BY CHANGING YOUR MARKET OR AUDIENCE POSITIONING

Suppose you currently define your authority based on having a certain number of subscribers. Consider your main competitor in the market, whose subscriber count stands at only 200,000. By positioning your metrics in close proximity to his level, shown by the second dotted line 'target authority' in Fig.5, you effectively alter the threshold you aim to achieve. Depending upon how big this shift is from your current position, it will determine how soon you can reach there. If you set meager metrics, you surely can reach there sooner. However, that target must have a rationale for establishing your authority at a certain level.

This shift can significantly reduce the time required to establish your authority. Once you set that 'target authority' definition in the form of metrics, this may take some time to achieve. The acceleration of authority development also relies on your niche market. By recalibrating those metrics, you can expedite your progress. Imagine narrowing down your target audience to 100,000 students from a pool of millions. By defining a specific and focused market, the time it takes to reach that 100,000 becomes considerably shorter. Consequently, your authority can be attained in a more accelerated manner.

This highlights the crucial role of market positioning and audience targeting to determine the speed of accelerating the desired level of authority. Your market or audience positioning determines how soon or late you will reach your desired authority. It is essential to operate within a narrow market to establish your authority more rapidly.

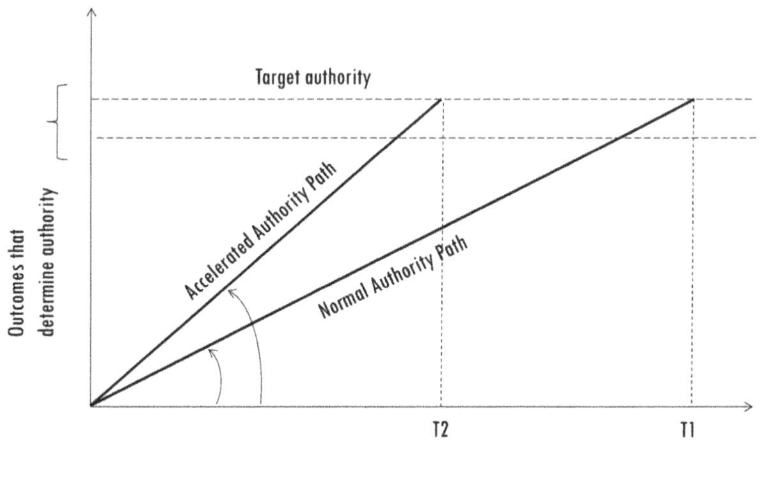

Figure 5: Accelerating authority by scoping the definition of success for a given market or audience positioning

BY USING YOUR PROFESSIONAL NICHE AS A HEADSTART

Let's now dig into another aspect: Gaining a headstart in your journey toward authority. This advantage can be obtained through a professional niche. When your niche is well-defined, distinct, and accompanied by a clear sense of purpose, you position yourself ahead of others in commencing your journey.

The beauty of a headstart lies in the fact that even if you progress at the same pace as others, you will still reach your target authority in a shorter time frame.

Figure 6: Accelerating authority by getting a headstart with a sharply defined micro-niche

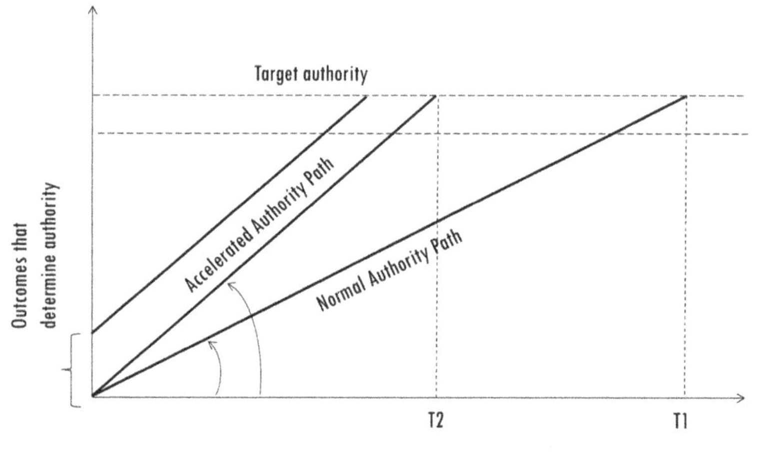

By establishing a professional niche that is both focused and refined, you set yourself apart from the competition right from the beginning. This early advantage provides you with a significant edge in your quest for authority, allowing you to achieve your goals in a more expeditious manner.

BY LEVERAGING YOUR DOCUMENTED WISDOM

Now, let's address another crucial aspect: Advancing along the 'accelerated authority path,' which signifies your path forward. How can you accelerate your journey? It all hinges on the documentation of your wisdom. Consider this: Have you meticulously recorded the extensive wisdom you have amassed over the years? Is it captured in a book or highlighted through articles published in reputable magazines? Are your profound insights shared on authentic platforms that endure over time?

Here, I am not referring to the fleeting nature of social media, as its impact is merely a small fraction of overall success. Instead, I am emphasizing the importance of tangible elements—a book, articles, or other contributions—that serve as enduring evidence of your expertise in construction project management.

To establish yourself as an authority in the field, it is imperative to possess coherent wisdom. These concrete manifestations of your knowledge determine the speed at which you progress along your journey. They serve as testaments to your expertise and enable you to accelerate your path.

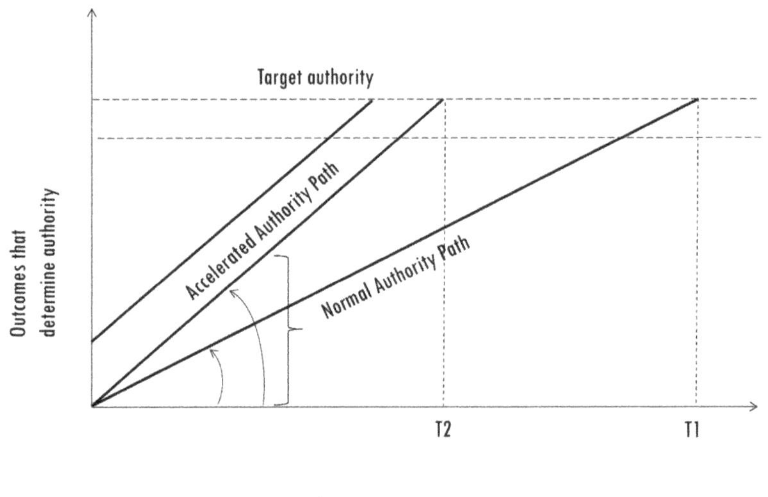

Figure 7: Accelerating authority by increasing the slope of the growth curve with documented wisdom

BY CREATING AN UNBEATABLE VALUE PROPOSITION

Let's focus on another piece of the puzzle: Your value proposition. As mentioned earlier, when your value proposition is incredibly compelling and unparalleled, it sets you apart from the competition. This holds tremendous significance in terms of accelerating your journey toward becoming an authority in your niche market.

Figure 8: Accelerating authority by compressing time with an unbeatable value proposition

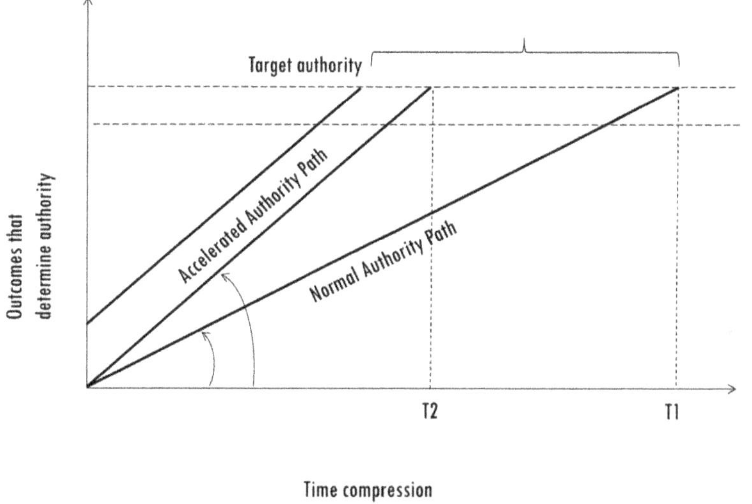

With a strong value proposition that is unrivaled, you gain a significant advantage, allowing you to establish authority at a much faster pace than anyone else. This is the key to achieving compression: Compressing the time it takes to ascend to the esteemed status of an authority in your field.

BY MAKING A STANDOUT IMPRESSION OR BRANDING

Let's now address the final aspect: Target authority. It all comes down to how effectively you differentiate yourself within your market, and this heavily relies on your impression or standout branding. Your impression and branding must resonate with your target audience and set you apart.

Figure 9: Accelerating authority by establishing a standout branding for the desired authority level

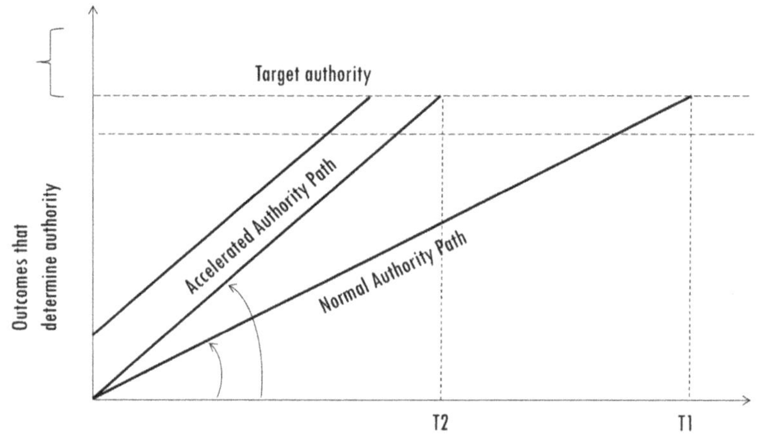

Here, I am not referring to building personal branding or simply posting on social media. It is about truly embodying who you are. By crafting a compelling and unique identity, you position yourself to stay ahead of the curve. It is about leaving a lasting impression that makes you remarkably distinctive.

TIP: DEFINE OUTCOMES FIRST

To establish and accelerate professional authority, focus on identifying a micro-niche where you excel, targeting a specific audience, creating a standout impression through branding and communication, sharing wisdom in tangible forms, and crafting an unbeatable value proposition. Integrating these components accelerates the journey toward expertise. However, too much focus on merely the process can be detrimental by taking away the time that could have been utilized more efficiently to map the outcomes. For such an accelerated process, it is extremely important to define the outcomes for each of the five elements of the *Accelerated Authority Development Framework* highlighted in this chapter. When outcomes are clear, you know what success looks like as an authority in your area. Then you can work backward to put everything in place to make it happen. This thorough definition of the outcomes in turn establishes a path toward refining the process even more, adding more speed to your progress.

6

Aligning Two Aspects of Niche

"To identify your niche, focus on the intersection of your passions, skills, and the needs of the market; it is here that your unique value lies."

- Chris Guillebeau, The $100 Startup: Reinvent the Way You Make a Living, Do What You Love, and Create a New Future

Identifying your niche is a crucial aspect of establishing yourself as an expert in your field. At the forefront of accelerating authority lies a crucial step: Identifying a professional niche that remains steadfast throughout one's life. Sally Hogshead, in Fascinate: Your 7 Triggers to Persuasion and Captivation, appeals, *"Find your micro-niche by identifying the unique qualities and insights that set you apart from others; be bold in claiming your space, and others will recognize your expertise."*

However, the process of identifying and solidifying this niche is far more challenging than it may appear. Our surroundings are inundated with an abundance of noise, particularly the noise we encounter on social media. We find ourselves inadvertently following the practices of our peers, colleagues, and acquaintances. Regrettably, this often leads to a sense of misplacement.

I have encountered numerous instances where individuals sought my guidance after straying from their own path due to blindly following those they trusted. The underlying issue lies in navigating this clamor and successfully aligning not only the expertise niche but also the market niche. This alignment is key to setting one's unique niche within the crowded and saturated market.

ALIGNING EXPERTISE AND MARKET NICHE

To differentiate yourself from the millions of other experts out there, it is important to understand and then align the two aspects of your niche: Expertise niche and market niche.

Expertise niche: Your unique skill set

The first element of your niche revolves around your expertise, which encompasses your specialty, unique area of knowledge, or strongest skill set. This is what distinguishes you from others and makes you truly indispensable. However, it is essential to be mindful that if you do not handle it well, others might eventually be able to imitate your niche. To establish a robust expertise niche, it is crucial to possess a profound understanding of your strengths, skills, and passions.

For instance, if you work as an engineer, your expertise niche could be centered around developing software specifically designed for the automotive industry. This becomes your unique selling point, setting you apart from other professionals in your field who may not specialize in this specific domain. By focusing on this niche, you position yourself as an expert within your industry, becoming a longed-for resource for advice and guidance in this particular area.

Market niche: Your target audience

Another important aspect of your niche involves defining your market or target audience. This aspect focuses on identifying the individuals or groups you aim to serve. Your target audience could encompass businesses, consumers, students, professionals, executives, or even a specific age group or industry type.

To illustrate, let's consider the previous example of your niche expertise in developing software for the automotive industry. In this case, your market niche may revolve around targeting business-to-business (B2B) clients within the automotive sector. By directing your efforts toward a specific market, you can customize your offerings and messaging to cater to the needs and preferences of that audience. This approach facilitates the establishment of your expertise in their eyes, as you align closely with their specific requirements.

TIP: HONE BOTH NICHES

It is worth emphasizing that both your expertise and market niches require continuous refinement and clarification through an iterative thought process. By developing a strong comprehension of both aspects, you can position yourself as an expert who possesses not only in-depth knowledge and proficiency in a particular area but also the ability to provide targeted solutions to the specific issues and obstacles encountered by your target audience. In conclusion, the identification and refinement of both aspects of your niche allow you to establish yourself as a sought-after expert with valuable expertise. This differentiation will enable you to distinguish yourself from others and attain professional success at an accelerated pace.

7

Identifying Compelling Micro-Niche

"In identifying your micro-niche, remember that your unique perspective and experiences are your greatest asset; embrace your individuality and use it to stand out in your space."

- Austin Kleon, Show Your Work! 10 Ways to Share Your Creativity and Get Discovered

Reid Hoffman, co-founder of LinkedIn, offers valuable insight pointing to the need to establish micro-niche authority. He states, *"The key to success is to focus on a niche that you can dominate."* This focus involves providing tailored solutions catering to the specific needs of a carefully identified target audience. By narrowing the scope of professional offerings to a niche, one can situate oneself as the go-to authority or primary choice.

My background as an engineer, immersed in scientific research and product development, has imparted a pivotal lesson: The scientific and technological domains maintain a distinct advantage due to their perpetual focus on a niche. Within these fields, there exists a systematic array of tools, techniques, and methods that enable individuals to identify, specify, clarify, and effectively communicate their expertise. This specialization adds fathomable value to their end customers, propelling their professional success with matchless speed.

Let us take a look at two individuals who found success by identifying and establishing their own professional niches.

Marie Forleo, a life coach and author, started off as a life coach but realized there was an opportunity in the market for coaching that combined spirituality with practical business strategies. By focusing on this unique niche, she set herself apart from others in her industry and became recognized as an authority.

Another example is Tim Ferriss, an entrepreneur and author who specializes in self-improvement and productivity. He gained fame for creating a system that helps people optimize their personal and business lives. His success has made him a respected figure in the field of personal development. Both Marie Forleo and Tim Ferriss demonstrate the importance of finding a specialized area of expertise to stand out and achieve professional success.

USE WHAT YOU ALREADY HAVE

When it comes to identifying your niche, you are often presented with two options. The first option involves utilizing your existing expertise to carve out a niche, which can be a relatively quicker path. On the other hand, the second option requires starting from scratch, especially when you lack a defined niche or aim to enter a different field. This latter option is time-consuming and can be challenging for many professionals. It demands more time and energy compared to leveraging what you already possess. Furthermore, it is also the space where mistakes are commonly made. Instead of leveraging their existing skills and expertise, people might fall into the trap of following others' misguided advice, leading them astray from their intended path.

Therefore, my foremost advice is to prioritize leveraging your existing skills, knowledge, and experience rather than reinventing the wheel and impeding your progress toward establishing professional authority. This is especially crucial if you have spent 20-30 years building expertise in your specific career field. Even if the niche you plan to enter is not directly related to your prior area of expertise, you can still use this very expertise to lay a solid foundation and distinguish yourself even from the experts in this new field who might lack the rich background you bring from your previous career journey.

Elizabeth Gilbert, in Big Magic: Creative Living Beyond Fear, rightfully said, *"Identifying your niche is a journey of self-discovery; embrace the process and be open to change as you learn more about yourself and your passions."* In fact, some of the most successful experts in their fields have capitalized on their existing expertise and skills to establish their niche. For instance, Tim Ferriss leveraged his knowledge of technology, startups, and financing to establish himself as a productivity and lifestyle expert. Similarly, Marie Forleo leveraged her background in marketing, web design, and spirituality to establish her niche as a personal development expert.

In conclusion, harnessing what you already possess can speed up establishing your niche and distinguish you in your field. By utilizing your existing expertise, skills, and experience, you can bypass the time and effort required to start from scratch, swiftly positioning yourself as an authority in your chosen domain.

5-E THINKING PROCESS TO FIND COMPELLING MICRO-NICHE

The 5-E Thinking Process presents a structured approach to discovering and establishing a specialized professional micro-niche. This framework comprises five essential components: Experience, Expertise, Ecosystem, Energy, and Efforts. By carefully evaluating and incorporating these elements, individuals can create a distinct niche aligned with their specific talents, passions, and potential avenues for success.

Figure 10: The 5-E system of identifying micro-niche

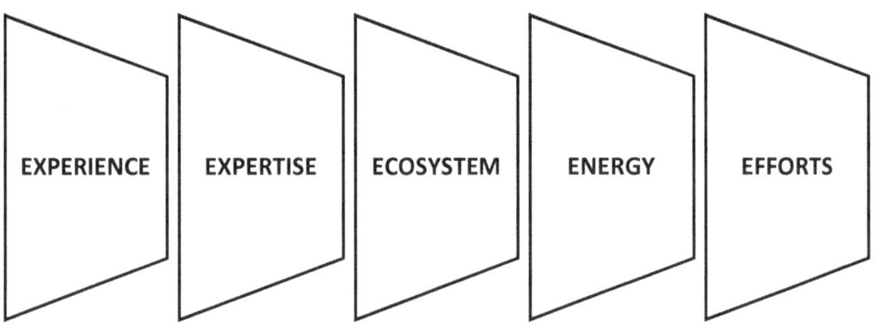

Table 6: Significance of each element of the 5-E system

Criteria	Signifies
EXPERIENCE	BREADTH
EXPERTISE	DEPTH
ECOSYSTEM	LEVERAGES
ENERGY	MOTIVATION
EFFORTS	EFFICIENCY

When embarking on a new venture within a specific field, it is beneficial to assess multiple micro-niches within that field. To begin with, identify 2-3 micro-niches you are contemplating. For instance, if your interest lies in technical design, you may have experience and knowledge in various subfields such as construction project management, software engineering, or product design. To determine the most suitable micro-niche, conducting a comprehensive evaluation using the *5-E Thinking Process* can be helpful.

Begin by listing the different micro-niches under consideration, assigning each one a name that accurately represents the specific area of interest. In the following sections, you will use a framework to evaluate and score the best micro-niche that can make you shine as a top-notch authority.

EXPERIENCE

Your experience forms the foundation upon which you build your niche. It provides you with a **breadth** of knowledge and insights that give you a solid platform to stand on. Having diverse experiences across different companies or ventures allows you to gather a breadth of expertise, providing you with a broader perspective and a strong base from which to launch your specialized niche.

One way to identify, define and gauge breadth your experience is by creating a comprehensive inventory some of the following elements in a given micro-niche are:

- Domains

- Disciplines

- Career paths

- Past positions

- Job titles

- Offices held

- Volunteer roles

- Memberships

- Education

- Research

By leveraging this compilation, you can harness your accumulated knowledge and skills to carve out a specialized space for yourself in the professional realm.

Table 7: Identifying the strongest micro-niche based on the strongest experience

Experience (score each cell on a scale of 1 to 10)	Qualifying entries	Micro-niche #1	Micro-niche #2	Micro-niche #3	Micro-niche #4
Domains	DM1, DM2, DM3				
Disciplines	D1, D2, D3				
Career paths	C1, C2, C3				
Past positions	P1, P2, P3				
Job titles	J1, J2, J3				
Offices held	O1, O2, O3				
Volunteer roles	V1, V2, V3				
Memberships	M1, M2, M3				
Education	E1, E2, E3				
Research	R1, R2, R3				
High scorer niche					

You need to evaluate your overall experience deeply to figure out the **strongest experience** that will help you identify the most promising micro-niche to develop further. The key assessment question is - *How Well Is Your Potential Niche Connected with Your Broader Experience?*

To effectively evaluate the experience across various micro-niches, it is important to delve deeper into each one. Begin by examining and identifying under which domain each micro-niche falls, considering the different areas of work you have been involved in. For example, one micro-niche may align with a specific domain, while another may pertain to a different one. As you assess each micro-niche, consider the evidence of your past positions, job titles, and roles within those domains. This examination will reveal whether you have tangible proof of working within a particular micro-niche.

It is crucial to determine if you hold a job title that directly corresponds to each micro-niche. Take note of any micro-niche where you lack a job title that reflects your involvement in that specific area. This observation highlights the absence of concrete evidence supporting your experience in that micro-niche. By scrutinizing these aspects, you can assign scores to each criterion on a scale of 1 to 10, allowing for a comprehensive evaluation of your overall experience in each micro-niche.

Through this evaluation process, you gain a clearer understanding of the strength of your experience in different micro-niches. The objective is to identify the micro-niche that emerges as the highest scorer based on the criteria of domains, disciplines, career paths, past positions, job titles, offices held, volunteer roles, memberships, education, and research. This approach provides a comprehensive overview and assists in determining the micro-niche with the strongest foundation of experience.

EXPERTISE

"Expertise is the foundation upon which authority is built; without a deep understanding of your field, your influence will be short-lived and superficial."

- Malcolm Gladwell, Outliers: The Story of Success

Building upon your experience, your expertise is the key that unlocks the **depth** of your niche. Among your varied experiences, it is crucial to identify the specific area where you possess exceptional knowledge and skills. This expertise defines the depth of your niche and sets you apart as an authority in your chosen field. It is this specialization that enables you to offer unique solutions and valuable insights to your target audience.

Some of the elements that can help you determine the depth of your expertise in a given micro-niche are:

- Expertise

- Competence

- Outcomes

- Credentials

- Awards

- Features

- Credibility

- Content

- Books

- Articles

- Research

- Models

To begin, it is essential to identify and evaluate your areas of expertise, focusing on the two or three domains where your skills surpass those of your peers and anyone else within your professional field. The level of competence you possess in these areas is crucial.

Additionally, the outcomes you have achieved play a significant role in establishing your expertise. For instance, if a surgeon consistently achieves a 97% success rate in operations, he is considered an expert in his field. Therefore, the results you deliver are vital indicators of your expertise.

Furthermore, your credentials, such as certificates, awards, and recognition, contribute to your credibility as an expert. Factors like working for a renowned company or having clients from reputable organizations enhance your credibility too. It is important to compile a comprehensive list of such credentials.

The content you have produced, including books or research, also serves to establish you as an expert. Sharing your knowledge and insights through these mediums further solidifies your expertise in your chosen micro-niche.

Table 8: Identifying the strongest micro-niche based on the most verifiable expertise

Expertise (score each cell on a scale of 1 to 10)	Micro-niche #1	Micro-niche #2	Micro-niche #3	Micro-niche #4
Top Expertise				
Top Competence				
Top Accomplishments				
Top Credentials				

High scorer niche				
Top Models				
Top Research				
Top Articles				
Top Books				
Top Content				
Top Credibility				
Top Features				
Top Awards				

You need to evaluate your overall expertise extensively to figure out the **verifiable expertise** that helps you identify the most promising micro-niche. The key assessment question is - *What evidence do you have that supports the criteria?*

Let's now shift our focus to evaluating expertise, which is a straightforward process revolving around verifiable evidence. Without concrete evidence, it becomes challenging to establish your authority. So, what exactly does evidence entail? It should be verifiable and can come in various forms, such as awards, features, certificates, testimonials, credentials, published works, endorsements, and more. When examining each micro-niche, consider the top areas where you possess expertise. Are there verifiable evidences, testimonials, or certificates to support your claim? Ensure you list down this evaluation across all the micro-niches.

By performing this exercise, you gain insight into the micro-niche with the most substantial evidence. These are the areas where you possess a wealth of verifiable evidence. Imagine the impact this will have when you establish your authority through a website or other platforms. You can display the evidence to support your claims. This collection of evidence solidifies your status as a global authority in that particular micro-niche. However, without evidence, it would be a lofty assertion. This systematic approach enables you to make informed decisions and establish your authority with credibility.

For instance, in the micro-niche of digital marketing, having a Google AdWords certificate, client testimonials, and being published in a reputable marketing magazine can solidify one's credibility. However, lacking verifiable evidence in such a specific micro-niche means it is not appropriate to claim expertise in that area. Tangible evidence is the key to establishing professional authority.

ECOSYSTEM

"Creating an ecosystem of support and mutual growth will not only elevate your authority but also the authority of those around you."

- Reid Hoffman, The Startup of You: Adapt

The ecosystem surrounding your niche plays a critical role in its establishment. By evaluating the opportunities and **leverages** within your environment, you can strategically position yourself to build a strong and sustainable niche. Understanding the dynamics of the market, identifying potential collaborations, and recognizing the needs of your audience will enable you to tap into existing resources and forge valuable connections, strengthening your niche and enhancing your chances of success.

Some of the elements that you can leverage from your ecosystem to build an unbeatable micro-niche are:

- Followers

- Subscribers

- Connections

- Clients

- Leverages

- Opportunities

- Engagements

- Memberships

- Forums

When aspiring to become an authority in a specific domain, it is imperative to assess the resources at your disposal. For instance, you may possess a thriving YouTube channel with a substantial subscriber base. However, if this is not the case, alternative avenues need to be explored.

Take a moment to consider the individuals within your network. Who are your connections, friends, and clients? Have you rendered your services and forged meaningful relationships? Moreover, consider the demographics of the individuals you have served. Have your interactions primarily revolved around the tech industry? If that is the case, the tech realm presents a promising opportunity to establish your niche.

Then again, it is crucial to scrutinize your LinkedIn profile. When was the last time you thoroughly assessed its contents? LinkedIn provides valuable insights, indicating the industries and job roles represented within your connections. It reveals the percentage of CEOs, managers, and project managers in your network. Identifying any gaps in your LinkedIn connections, especially when targeting a niche related to students, highlights missed opportunities. Leveraging what you already possess is an integral part of establishing your authority.

Furthermore, it is essential to evaluate the engagement and opportunities available within your ecosystem. Are you an active member of relevant forums where you can participate and showcase your expertise? These elements form a crucial part of the ecosystem that surrounds you.

Table 9: Identifying the strongest micro-niche based on the best leverages available in the ecosystem

Ecosystem (score each cell on a scale of 1 to 10)	Micro-niche #1	Micro-niche #2	Micro-niche #3	Micro-niche #4
Followers				
Subscribers				
Connections				
Clients				
Leverages				
Opportunities				
Engagements				

Memberships				
Forums				
High scorer niche				

To identify the most efficacious micro-niche, you need to figure out the **best leverages** by deeply evaluating your overall ecosystem. The key assessment question is - *What leverages do you have in each potential niche?*

To make informed decisions, it is crucial to adopt a comprehensive and systematic approach to evaluating micro-niches. By considering both your experience and expertise alongside the ecosystem of each niche, you can determine which areas hold the greatest potential for success. This strategic assessment allows you to channel your efforts effectively and optimize your chances of achieving desired outcomes.

ENERGY

Your energy fuels the drive and **motivation** to excel in your chosen niche. It is the force that propels you forward, pushing you to become an expert in your particular area. Your genuine passion and motivation for your niche will keep you engaged and inspired, even during challenging times. Harnessing this energy and aligning it with your aspirations will give you the resilience and dedication needed to overcome obstacles and continuously grow within your niche.

Some of the elements that determine the level of energy you invest in a given micro-niche are:

- Motivators

- Dreams

- Drivers

- Passions

- Why

- What for

- Power Story

- Successes

Ask yourself the following questions - What drives and motivates you? What are your aspirations and dreams? Is your current pursuit aligned with your past endeavors, or does it encompass something entirely new? Envision a scenario where you are embarking on a completely novel journey, pursuing a dream you have never experienced before.

In such instances, starting from scratch becomes inevitable as you construct your niche and establish your authority. Therefore, it is crucial to have a clear understanding of your motivators within your chosen niche. Moreover, the power of storytelling cannot be overstated.

Imagine a future where you have attained the status of an authority in your field. The question arises: Do I possess an impactful personal story that commands attention? Take for example, I share my own narrative when I interact with others. When I go out, I tell people that I cannot walk but I am going to teach you how to walk faster. That is my story, and it resonates powerfully. People cannot disregard it because they witness my transformation from a physical limitation to an unwavering focus on speed. Through relentless dedication, I have mastered the art of speed and now I aim to guide others on their own path to mastery. Such a story holds immense significance and cannot be overlooked.

Just imagine the potency that arises when your niche emerges from such a compelling narrative. It becomes an irresistible force. Often, individuals struggle to define their niche clearly until they embrace the power of a captivating story. Without a compelling narrative, many individuals struggle to define their niche with clarity. By infusing your niche with a powerful story, you harness its remarkable potential and create a force that cannot be ignored.

Table 10: Identifying the strongest micro-niche based on sources of your perpetual energy and motivation

Energy (score each cell on a scale of 1 to 10)	**Micro-niche #1**	**Micro-niche #2**	**Micro-niche #3**	**Micro-niche #4**
Followers				
Subscribers				
Connections				
Clients				
Leverages				
Opportunities				
Engagements				
Memberships				
Forums				
High scorer niche				

To identify the most auspicious micro-niche, you need to figure out the **perpetual motivation** by thoroughly evaluating your overall motivations and drivers. The key assessment question is - *Who can vouch for your drivers for the potential niche?*

Let's discuss your energy and motivators. This aspect is quite fascinating as it encompasses your dreams, drivers, and passions toward a particular micro-niche. You may say, "I have been dreaming of pursuing this work for as long as I can remember." Now, who can validate this? Can your father vouch for your childhood discussions about this passion? Or perhaps your spouse observed your unwavering dedication to this specific pursuit. These personal connections can serve as witnesses, attesting to your genuine passion and commitment to the micro-niche.

By involving your family, you tap into the emotional aspect associated with your energy and motivators. Their perspective may differ from your own, revealing a more objective picture. Ultimately, establishing authority is about visibility and perception. If your family members, including your spouse, parents, or siblings, do not perceive your passion, drivers, and power story within that particular niche, it is likely that your audience will find it hard to believe as well. After all, if your own family cannot see it, convincing others becomes a challenge.

This objective evaluation process mirrors the product development cycle within a niche. It involves constructive criticism and the clash of great minds, ultimately leading to the creation of the best products on the market.

EFFORTS

Effort and **efficiency** are crucial factors to consider when establishing a niche. Becoming an expert or authority in a specific field requires not only dedicated effort but also a focus on efficiency. You need to assess the time and resources required to attain the level of expertise you desire within your niche while also finding ways to optimize your efforts.

Some of the elements that communicate the level of effort you need to put in are:

- Content

- Research

- Models

- Bandwidth

- Challenges

- Acceptability

- Successes

- Audience

- Opportunities

It is crucial to consider the time and effort required to carve out a niche for yourself. Rather than embarking on a path that demands two decades of arduous journeying, it is helpful to leverage existing content and experiences. Perhaps you have authored articles or completed projects that have bestowed you with invaluable expertise. This reservoir of knowledge can be harnessed immediately, sparing you from reinventing the wheel. It is vital to capitalize on what you already possess.

Furthermore, an essential aspect to consider is the level of acceptance your business or services will receive in today's landscape. Will people readily embrace and adopt what you have to offer? Having a network of friends and acquaintances who will readily take advantage of your services can significantly reduce the effort required. Opting for a path that aligns with established relationships and promptly welcomes acceptance becomes the desirable course of action.

Efficiency and efficacy are key considerations when establishing professional authority within a micro-niche. By leveraging existing resources and tapping into a network of readily accepting individuals, you can streamline your efforts and accelerate your path to success.

Table 11: Identifying the strongest micro-niche based on the ready-to-go credentials and least efforts

Efforts (score each cell on a scale of 1 to 10)	Micro-niche #1	Micro-niche #2	Micro-niche #3	Micro-niche #4
Content				
Research				
Models				
Bandwidth				
Challenges				
Acceptability				
Successes				
Audience				
Opportunities				
High scorer niche				

You need to thoroughly evaluate your resources and accomplishments to figure out the **ready-to-go credentials** that will help you identify the most promising micro-niche to develop further. The key assessment question is - *What is your readiness for your potential niche?*

The final step in evaluating your micro-niche is to assess your dedication and readiness. This involves examining how much effort has been dedicated toward factors such as content creation, research endeavors, establishing models or frameworks, and tackling challenges. It is crucial to evaluate whether you have dedicated the right kind of efforts; this can be in the form of writing a book or conducting research in the micro-niche, possessing applicable models or frameworks, and having the necessary time and resources to commit to it. Additionally, considering potential challenges and your acceptance of them is essential.

For instance, if your aspiration is to establish a business within a specific micro-niche, you must determine if you can dedicate the required time and resources. This entails developing a business plan, conducting market research, and devising effective strategies to engage your target audience. If you lack the necessary commitment or resources, it may be wise to reconsider your choice of micro-niche or explore alternative opportunities.

To assess your readiness, it is crucial to be honest with yourself about your level of commitment and the resources at your disposal. This self-reflection will enable you to make informed decisions about whether you are prepared to pursue a particular micro-niche and how you can allocate your resources effectively to achieve your goals.

FINDING COMPELLING MICRO-NICHE

Utilize a 1-to-10 scaling system to rate your experience in each niche. A score of 10 signifies exceptional experience, while a score of 1 indicates limited exposure. Consider factors such as the duration of your involvement in each niche, the level of expertise you have attained, and any specialized skills you have acquired. Beyond evaluating your experience in each micro-niche, it is crucial to consider your ecosystem of connections and motivation. Assess the number of LinkedIn connections you have within each niche and reflect upon which one elicits the greatest sense of energy and motivation. These factors play a pivotal role in networking and succeeding within your chosen field, warranting their consideration.

By conducting a thorough self-assessment of your experience, expertise, ecosystem, energy, and efforts pertaining to each micro-niche, you can gain valuable insights into the ideal fit for your professional pursuits. This process enables you to identify the micro-niche with the highest scores, serving as the focal point for your future endeavors and growth.

Table 12: Identifying the strongest micro-niche based on all the five elements of 5-E system

5E elements	Micro-niche #1	Micro-niche #2	Micro-niche #3	Micro-niche #4
Experience				
Expertise				
Energy				
Ecosystem				
Efforts				
SCORES				
High scorer niche				

TIP: INTEGRATING ALL SCORING TOGETHER

By employing the above criteria-driven evaluation and scoring model across the five key areas, you can discover a micro-niche that shines above the rest. It will become evident which micro-niche holds an abundance of experience, expertise, and compelling evidence, supported by the testimony of your family's recognition of your passion, along with leverages within your ecosystem, and readiness in the form of dedicated efforts toward a particular micro-niche. This process enables you to swiftly identify the most favorable micro-niche without the need for expensive consultants, social media influence, or costly programs that drain your finances. As a consequence, accelerating your journey toward identifying the most compelling micro-niche.

8

Developing Your Micro-Niche Story

"Leverage the power of storytelling to establish yourself as an authority; a compelling narrative will resonate with your audience and solidify your expertise."

- Carmine Gallo, Talk Like TED: The 9 Public-Speaking Secrets of the World's Top Minds

WHY DEVELOP AN AUTHORITY STORY

What makes you an authority in your micro-niche? You will need a compelling answer to this simple but profound question almost everywhere. You need it as part of the pitch for a speaking gig, a book publishing proposal, bidding for a project, or applying for a media feature. Often, experts do not have a great handle on this answer.

For that, you need to build an "authority story" that explains how you uncovered or discovered your micro-niche, how you developed your expertise, how your passions fuel it, and how you identified a gap in the market that you aim to serve using your expertise. That story presents your journey, how you accumulated experience, credentials, projects, achievements, and successes while serving toward that aim, and how it shaped your authority.

Just like the brand story, it makes a personal connection with your audience or sponsors. You come across as a relatable person who has genuine reasons to share his expertise and who genuinely stands out as a distinct authority in his space.

Your authority story serves as the glue that binds your message together, bringing coherence and consistency to your communication with your audience. It acts as a powerful tool to articulate your vision and goals, resonating with your target audience on a deeper level. Therefore, crafting a thoughtful and concise narrative that effectively conveys your passion and dedication to your chosen niche is paramount.

HOW TO DEVELOP YOUR AUTHORITY STORY

By crafting a well-rounded authority story, you have the ability to inspire, engage, and captivate your audience. You can now establish yourself as a respected leader and a catalyst for thought-provoking discussions within your micro-niche. With your authority story as your beacon, you will forge meaningful connections, build trust, and position yourself as a trusted expert in your field.

Keep in mind that your story needs to answer three things:

1. How did your authority originate in the first place?

2. How has your authority developed over time?

3. How is your authority uniquely positioned to help you?

Here is an example of my authority story which I can use on a media one-sheeter, as part of my introduction, as a speaker introduction by the host, and several other things. It integrates events, drivers, outcomes, and specialization all into one.

Walking the accelerated learning path, I have earned over 100 international degrees and educational credentials–which include 2 Doctorates, 3 Master's degrees, and tens of Diplomas and Certificates. I have been nominated for some of the world's highest certifications. With my two practice-based doctorates and specialized research, I am one of the few experts in the world who have figured out how to reduce time to mastery by 50%. I walk the talk as an accelerated learning scientist.

While I had experienced the risks of not being able to go to school, I have been awarded 2 doctorates and have earned over 100+ international and educational credentials, including 3 master's degrees, several PGDs, diplomas, and certifications.

As the world's leading authority on speed in learning, performance, professional development, and leadership, I deliver research-based insights to leaders on making "speed" a priority. In guiding them on how to design the whole ecosystem to accelerate employee development during accelerated times, I offer exclusive know-how in organizational and personal space.

Leveraging every dimension of my multi-faceted personality, I write about the deeper aspects of human excellence and capabilities. I have authored over 20 multi-genre books and several research papers, covering a range of disciplines from engineering, science, leadership, management, training, learning, performance, and as diverse topics as the arts, poetry, and painting. I bring in-depth experiences, stories, and case studies from different walks of life.

My professional career and experience span over 25 years in various domains. Qualified as an engineer, I have worked in the technical and technology fields for a decade. Alongside this, I received project and program management opportunities while managing operations. Later, I embedded myself in the world of training, learning, and performance. I have acquired experience in 8 diverse disciplines over the course of my professional career. My multidisciplinary and multidomain experience allows me to bring the highest level of value and context to my solutions.

Expertise does not deliver value unless it is explicitly seen by the world. I have been showcased in over 125 media features that include TV interviews, radio interviews, magazine feature stories, podcasts, and hundreds of citations or mentions of my thought leadership across a spectrum of outlets. I appeared on the covers of some of the magazines apart from being featured in their interviews.

DEVELOPING YOUR AUTHORITY STORY

When developing your authority story, keep in mind the key elements that make it impactful:

- **Passion**: Clearly articulate why your micro-niche captivates you and fuels your enthusiasm to invest your time and energy into it.
- **Expertise and Experience**: Showcase what sets you apart from others in your niche, highlighting the unique skills, knowledge, and achievements you have acquired over time.
- **Vision and Goals**: Share your aspirations and the meaningful impact you hope to make by dedicating yourself to this niche. Paint a compelling picture of the future you envision and how it aligns with the needs of your audience.
- **Motivation**: Unveil the driving force behind your relentless pursuit of your passion within this micro-niche, providing insight into the personal and professional motivations that fuel your journey.

TIP: KEEP IT ALIVE

Remember, your authority story is a dynamic narrative that evolves alongside your journey. Continuously refine and adapt it as you gain new experiences, insights, and achievements within your micro-niche. Embrace the power of storytelling and watch as your authority grows, establishing you as a true force to be reckoned with in your specialized domain.

9

Career Acceleration Resources

LEARN FROM POWER-PACKED BOOKS

Accelerate your training thought leadership! Purchase these books at **amazon.com/author/raman.k.attri**.

Chief Learning Technology Officer in the Era of Speed

Written for senior learning technology leaders who want to shine as CXO executives. This book describes five strategies to leverage current technologies to shorten time-to-proficiency and provides leaders with a framework to evaluate future technologies to impact employee development speed. You will walk out with an integrated system thinking about measuring, tracking, and reducing time-to-proficiency while integrating time-to-proficiency metrics as technology KPIs

Chief e-Learning Officer in the Era of Speed

Written for senior e-learning and training leaders who want to shine as CXO executives. The book describes five strategies to institute breakthrough e-learning to shorten time-to-proficiency. This book provides multi-level tips and operational tactics to implement these strategies. You will walk out with an integrated system thinking about a holistic e-learning ecosystem, which indeed can shorten time-to-proficiency metrics.

Iconic Chief Learning Officer

Written for visionary training and learning leaders to guide them through a breakthrough framework to become a globally recognized iconic chief learning officer. This book teaches the art and science of impactful corporate learning leadership above and beyond your job and your organization. Learn the secrets of accelerating your career to unimaginable heights.

Releasing 2024

How to Plan Your Doctorate Journey Smartly

Written for aspiring working professionals and practitioners, this book is a complete guide for getting started to take up a PhD/doctorate program. If you are at a turning-point stage in your corporate or management career, where you are actively thinking of attaining the highest level of educational degree to create that extra edge in your career, then this book is for you. This book will provide you with key strategies to address behind-the-scenes challenges and complete your doctorate with reasonably less efforts. In this book, you will be able to identify the skills, competencies, and expertise required to undertake successful doctorate research, leverage your current and previous practice-based experience and translate that into doctorate research.

ENROLL IN ONLINE TRAINING COURSES

Accelerate your learning, training, and technology leadership with the following powerful online courses. For more such courses, head out to **get-there-faster.com/courses**.

L&D Leader and Strategist: Your Learning Leadership Accelerated

The learning, training, and development space is overcrowded and highly competitive now. Establishing yourself as a distinguished L&D leader is not easy anymore. You need to adopt a specific thought process and proven strategies to speed up your path to becoming a top L&D leader with unique specialization, positioning, and credibility. In this online course, learn the science of accelerating the path to becoming a top-notch learning and training leader. Master strategies, methods, and frameworks to put yourself onto the world map at an accelerated rate.

Enroll at **get-there-faster.com/learning-leadership-course**

Speed Learner: Accelerated Learning Skill in the Era of Speed

Have you ever wished to learn anything faster in your profession or business? You get overwhelmed by a humongous amount of content, tasks, activities, and projects to master. You do not know where to start. The end result is that it takes you a long time, sometimes years, to master everything you have to do in your job. You tried all possible methods, but you did not see a difference in your learning speed. More often, professionals and leaders are at a loss to set the appropriate goals for their speedier learning and then achieve them at a faster rate. In this course, you will gain breakthrough insights on how to position your approaches to learn faster for professional goals and set yourself apart from your peers. In this course, you will learn how someone is viewed as a fast learner by most organizations. In this course, you will learn a breakthrough technique from Dr. Raman to accelerate your learning for professional success in your profession or job.

Enroll at **get-there-faster.com/speed-learning-course**

Training Designer: Learn Powerful e-learning Design Practices to Speed Up Learning

Do you need to design online/e-learning courses to speed up the skill acquisition of your learners, but you don't know where to start? Life-changing skills are delivered when you design online or e-learning courses systematically using instructional design practices and using the latest and greatest strategies. In this training course, you will learn a new framework to think about your e-learning training design. You will walk out with proven, practical e-learning training design strategies from research used by some of the most advanced training organizations across the world. You will learn 3 key elements of e-learning design that you should pay attention to. You will also learn 5 strategies to make your e-learning courses powerful. You will adopt a new perspective on implementing 5 guiding principles in your e-learning or online courses.

Enroll at **get-there-faster.com/elearning-design-course**

Strategize Technologies to Speed Up Employee Development

The speed with which teams are developed is far more critical now to meet the challenges of complex next-generation projects amidst a fast-paced business environment. Technologies are now the first line of defense to impact how employees learn, develop, and perform at a workplace. In this revolutionary course, you will receive first-hand research-based wisdom on an integrated system thinking approach to measuring, tracking, and reducing time-to-proficiency using analytics strategically. You will acquire a renewed business acumen for marrying two things - 'workforce analytics' and 'time-to-proficiency metrics'- to build a people analytics strategy that can ensure improving employee performance faster. You will learn how futuristic-thinking organizations have leveraged state-of-the-art technologies, analytics, tools, and systems to shorten the time-to-proficiency of the workforce and teams at the speed of business.

Enroll at **get-there-faster.com/strategic-technologies-course**

Artificial Intelligence for Enterprise Learning

Are you an executive or enterprise leader looking to implement AI and ChatGPT in your organization? Look no further! In this FREE course, structured around real demos of 25 different elements of AI and ChatGPT for corporate applications, you will be taken through the evolution of this breakthrough technology. You will learn how AI and ChatGPT can revolutionize how your organization can design, develop, and manage large-scale training programs, e-learning solutions, and knowledge management processes. You will also see how ChatGPT can assist in writing procedures and managing your entire corporate e-learning and knowledge management supply chain. You will shake up your traditional thinking and open your mind about how you can take such a powerful tool to your upper management and shine as a visionary leader. Enroll at **get-there-faster.com/enterprise-ai**

GET CERTIFIED IN THE SCIENCE OF SPEED

Supercharge your learning leadership career to new heights by getting certified through a master certification program. For more such certifications, head out to **get-there-faster.com/pathways**.

Xcelerated Learning Strategist Certification: Speed-Savvy Chief Learning Officer

Designed for learning and training specialists, training managers, L&D professionals, human resources executives, and coaches to help them shine as world-class, speed-savvy learning thought leaders. This certification is awarded through rigorous training and qualification to develop the participants as the world's top-notch experts on accelerated learning in organizational space. Based on two decades of research, experience, experimentation, and authoring, this certification is structured around 5 power-packed tracks to qualify ambitious learning specialists who want to master the science of speed in learning, training, performance, and employee development.

To apply for acceptance to this certification, check out **get-there-faster.com/xcelerated-learning-guru-pathway.**

Xcelerated Training Design Guru Certification: Speed-Savvy Training Officer

Designed for learning and training specialists, training professionals, trainers, instructional designers, speakers, coaches, and teachers to help them shine as highly sought-after training design strategists. This certification is awarded through rigorous training and qualification to develop the participants as the world's top-notch experts in designing complex training and mentoring programs. If you need to equip your learners and audience with complex skills and improve their performance faster, then this advanced certification is for you. Based on two decades of research, experience, experimentation, and authoring, this certification is structured around 5 power-packed tracks to teach you the breakthrough, advanced, integrated methodologies for start-to-end analysis, design, development, and delivery of your training programs. Take your learning design to the next level by mastering the design of transformational coaching, mentoring, and certification programs.

To apply for acceptance to this certification, check out **get-there-faster.com/xcelerated-training-guru-pathway.**

INSIGHTFUL KEYNOTES FOR YOUR EVENTS

Interested to book me for powerful, insightful, research-backed, revolutionary keynotes and talks that will change your executives' thinking process? Then head on to **get-there-faster.com/speaking** and book me for your next corporate event. Book me and learn the science of acceleration to stay ahead in business!

FROM THE SAME AUTHOR

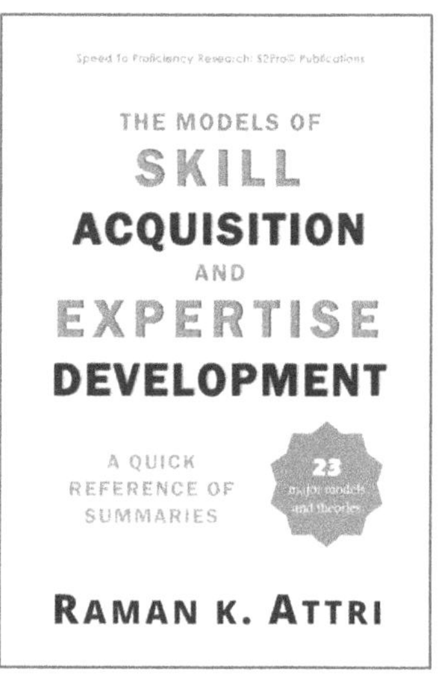

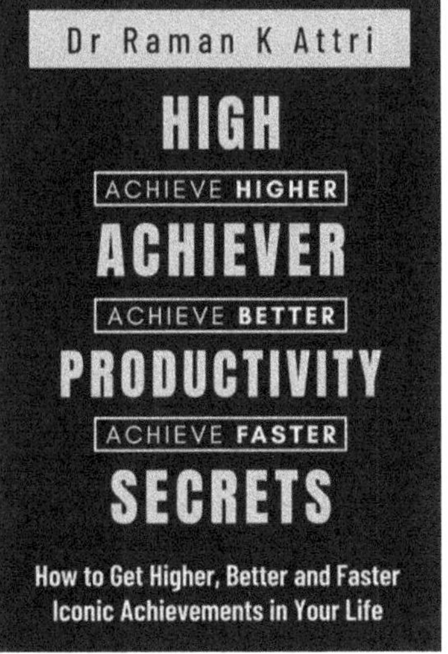

Dr Raman K Attri
HIGH
ACHIEVE HIGHER
ACHIEVER
ACHIEVE BETTER
PRODUCTIVITY
ACHIEVE FASTER
SECRETS
How to Get Higher, Better and Faster
Iconic Achievements in Your Life

Dr RAMAN K. ATTRI
ACCELERATED
PROFICIENCY
FOR
ACCELERATED
TIMES
A REVIEW OF KEY CONCEPTS
AND METHODS TO SPEED UP
PERFORMANCE
Speed To Proficiency Research: S2Pro© Publications

TRAINING
IMPACT
MEASUREMENT
ROI of Complex
Training Programs
Made Simple
DR RAMAN K ATTRI

AN AWARD-WINNING CORPORATE EMPLOYEE'S
GUIDE TO INCREDIBLE CAREER POSITIONING
KILL
YOUR JOB
first
10 SECRETS TO DEVELOP
ICONIC PERFORMANCE AND
GROWTH BEYOND YOUR JOB
DR RAMAN K ATTRI

ABOUT THE BOOK

In today's fast-paced world, establishing yourself as a distinguished authority in your domain or space in the shortest possible time is not only desirable but essential for your success. Prepare for a self-discovery process that goes beyond your expertise, brand authority, and personal branding to identify your true authority. "Micro Authority" is the book that unveils the thinking process of becoming a 'micro-authority,' a sought-after authority figure within a carefully defined micro-niche.

You will learn five powerful strategies from the *Accelerated Professional Authority Development Framework* to systematically identify and develop your professional micro-authority faster than your peers.

With science-based backing from a robust *Product Authority Model*, this book brings a well-researched *Professional Authority Model* to help you become a standout product in your space, paving your path to peak authority and branding.

What truly sets this book apart is its eye-opening insights that help you clarify the scope, breadth, and depth of your professional authority. The book equips you with a mechanism to define your authority metrics and help you prioritize them effectively to charter a future-proof trajectory toward becoming a go-to figure in your profession.

In a world where visibility is the currency, mastering your micro-niche is the key to making an unshakable standing in the business world. The book introduces a groundbreaking systems thinking approach to identify a compelling and unbeatable micro-niche with precision that magnifies your impact above and ahead of your competition.

"Micro Authority" is your indispensable companion if you are determined to seize control of your expertise, conquer your niche, and skyrocket your professional authority.

Are you ready to take your place as an authority in your space in the era of speed?